LISTEN TO THE GREEN

LUCI SHAW

Harold Shaw Publishers
Wheaton, Illinois

Grateful acknowledgement is made to the editors of the following periodicals, in which some of these poems first appeared: The Christian Herald, The Christian Reader, Christian Life, Christianity Today, Crux, Eternity, The Fish, HIS, Interest, Kodon, Ktaadn, Wheaton Alumni

"Royalty," "Of consolation," "Tithes," "Blindfold," "Triptych," and "But not forgotten" appeared in the anthology Adam Among the Television Trees, *© 1971 by Word Books, and are reprinted by permission.*

Design: Kathy Lay Burrows

Photo credits: John Shaw, cover; Don Ontiveros, pp. 10, 35; Kathy Lay Burrows, pp. 18, 64, 88; Jay Steinke, pp. 26, 39; Richard Ball, pp. 29, 62, 93; David Singer, pp. 41, 87; Luci Shaw, p. 45; Robert Mead, p. 48

Library of Congress Catalog Card Number: 75-165791

ISBN 0-87788-502-8

Printed in the United States of America.

Fourth printing, April, 1984

for Robin
love
without obligation

A Fore Word

A famous literary man once inquired what the difference is between a great poem like Paradise Lost *and a cookbook. What, he asked, do you learn from a cookbook? Something new, something you did not know before, on every page. What new facts do you learn from Milton's epic? None—none at all. Instead of any knowledge of things, what you gain from Milton is a growth in "sympathy with the infinite," an exercise in "the great moral capacities of man." A more recent critic, Mr. Bernard I. Bell, says that in poetry "more is revealed about the nature of man than in any but the most extraordinary prose," and he believes the reading of poetry is important as a pointer in the direction of sanity.*

In his old age, Charles Darwin lamented that his mind had become a sort of sausage machine for grinding factual observations into scientific systems. He said that had he been able to live his life over again he would have frequently read poetry and listened to music, because "the loss of these tastes is a loss of happiness, and may possibly be injurious to the intellect,

6

and more probably to the moral character."

Perhaps as much as at any time in history, our own period has taken on the character of cold practicality supported yet lamented by Darwin. We suffer from a mania of supposing that anything really true must be expressed in scientific terms. We have still to discover that nothing really good and true in a large human way can ever be fully expressed in any such terms. Consequently we find ourselves disjointed, filled with quick starts and repeatedly empty direction, much like the old lady who asked, "How do I know what I think until I hear what I say?" "Getting and spending," said Wordsworth, "we lay waste our lives." Never before has the material been so important; never before have people had so much; and never before have they been so unsettled and so unhappy.

One of my own lifelong pleasures has been living with young people not yet captured and therefore still able, at times at least, to attain a state of freshness, expectancy and wonder. It is in such soil that poetry becomes a possibility. Poetry comes out of a certain state of mind and spirit, but even with such a condition an actual poem may never result. I have seen hundreds who have tried to write, as indeed I believe almost every young person tries, but who have failed. Some have become versifiers, that is, they have attained a facility for making rhymes and turning commonplace ideas into meter. But very few ever succeed in writing poetry itself.

Luci Shaw is one of these. She has gone through the long discipline both of language and thought required of one who is to write truly. She belongs to those who are capable of making us see—see what we have in some degree or fashion always seen, yet never quite. Her mind is not only sensitive but tough. She has learned not just to scratch the ground but to plow deep. When she writes of a christmas tree, or a star, or a sonic boom, or a gull, or a garbage truck, we can, if we read with care, hear the voice of the infinite. When she writes of a Sunday morning in church, the very usualness of it becomes unusual. She knows, like a good poet, how to avoid gush and how to emphasize by understating, as when, in a poem on Jonah, she says, "the whale/did as he was told." She writes no phrase that she has not only thought about carefully but passed through the needle-eye of her sense for melody, word-shaping, and a lovely chaste exactness.

Clyde S. Kilby, Wheaton, Illinois

Contents

A Fore Word   6
But not forgotten   10
Circles   11
in a Botticelli print   12
living room   12
Rib cage   12
Slow passage—Teel's Island   14
Bride   15
Shine in the dark I   16
Shine in the dark II   16
Shine in the dark III   16
to the municipal incinerator   17
The flounder   19
Royalty   20
Bloodcount   20
Blindfold   22
new birth: heart spring   24
Chance   25
No backtrack, old Hansel   27
sonic boom   27
Sweet light, sweet love, sweet life   28
too much to ask   30
night through a frosty window   31
Parabola   32
light my candle   34
Seventh day   34
The celebration   37
Under the snowing   38
on eating a cake all by yourself   38
common ground   39
Perfect love banishes fear   40
Small song   42
Steadfast taper   42
Maple leaf—Lisle Arboretum—October 8   43
Of consolation   46

Moses reclothed   47
A Song for simplicity   49
Of elms and God   50
new view   51
Exit   52
Moses: Psalm XC   53
". . . for who can endure the day of his coming?"   54
Explorer   55
Two answers to poverty   56
Dial-a-prayer   57
Open   58
Seed   58
Arrested   59
Lucifer now   60
February 24 encounter   61
The revolutionary   62
Equation   65
Mary's song   66
to know him risen   67
to a young suicide   68
Hundredfold   69
Absolute-ly   70
the bright side   71
". . . for you are a mist"   72
Grave yard   73
Sunday morning   74
First flurry   75
Tithes   76
Made flesh   77
Step on it   78
Night's lodging   79
forecast   79
air craft   80
Coins   81
Freeway   82
Ever green   83
Stronghold   84
Lord, come and see   84
Miracle   86
Tryptich   88
Out of the woods   90
Reluctant prophet   91
The partaking   91

But Not Forgotten

Whether or not I find the missing thing
it will always be
more than my thought of it.
Silver-heavy, somewhere it winks
in its own small privacy
playing
the waiting game with me.

And the real treasures do not vanish.
The precious loses no value
in the spending.
A piece of hope spins out
bright, along the dark, and is not
lost in space;
verity is a burning boomerang;
love is out orbiting and will
come home.

Circles

I sing of circles, rounded things,
      apples and wreaths and wedding rings,
   and domes and spheres,
       and falling tears,
     well-rounded meals,
        water wheels,
     bottoms of bells
     or walled-in wells;
    rain dropping, golden in the air
         or silver on your shining hair;
    pebbles in pewter-colored ponds
      making circles, rounds on rounds;
  the curve of a repeating rhyme;
     the circle of the face of time.
Beyond these circles I can see
    the circle of eternity.

Does passing of each season fair
    make of the four a noble square?
No. For to each the others lend
  a cyclic, curving, rhythmic blend.
Remember, spring in summer gone
  comes round again. New spring comes on.

    The circle in the eagle's eye
  mirrors the circle of the sky,
the blue horizon, end to end,
     end to end,
    over earth's never-ending bend.

The arc of love from God to men
    orbiting, goes to him again.
  My love, to loving God above,
    captures *me* in the round of love.

in a botticelli print

i am a dot on
paper
a single simple
smallness
of one color
joining hands
with a million others
on the north edge of an
angel's eyelash
to show you a part of truth
with no words

living room

this mirror's the silver coolness
       in your eye
the closing door is your back's
       final turning
the darkened lamp is hope
       turned out
the coal in the grate's my heart
       still burning

Rib Cage

Jonah, you
and I were both signs
to unbelievers.

Learning the anatomy
of ships and sea animals the hard way—
from the inside
out—you counted (bumping your stubborn head)
the wooden beams and the great

curving bones
and left
your own heart unexplored.
And you were tough.
Twice, damp but undigested,
you were vomited. For you
it was the only
way out.

No, you wouldn't die.
Not even burial softened you
and, free of the dark sea prisons,
you were still
caged in yourself—trapped
in your own hard continuing rage
at me and Nineveh.

For three nights
and three days dark as night—
as dark as yours—
I charted the innards
of the earth. I too swam
in its skeleton, its raw underground.
A captive
in the belly of the world
(like the fish, prepared by God)
I felt the slow pulse at the monster's heart,
tapped its deep arteries, wrestled
its root sinews, was bruised
by the undersides of all
its cold bony stones.

Submerged,
I had to die, I had
to give in to it, I had to go
all the way down
before I could be freed
to live for you
and Nineveh.

Slow passage — Teel's Island*

Though now you ride the crest of the field
and rise to the seasonal
slow heaving of the earth,
the gulls are the same, and the
restless sky.
Under you, strong airs still push
the waves—salt grasses lifting darkly
to break in milkweed, yarrow, queen anne's lace.

Never, now, dolphins. Moles
are the travelers in your deeps.
Field mice and crickets dart
among the weedy shallows at your stern.
Lichens barnacle your beam.
Only the rains wet your grey shrunken wood.
Only wind slaps your sides.
The far barn's lightning rod
is the lone compass needle
to tell you your true north.
And oars I cannot see
pull, twist and feather
in your stiff rowlocks, to keep you
heading west.

Teel's Island is the title of Andrew Wyeth's painting, which
shows an old dinghy stranded high in a field.

Bride

The thin smooth eggshell of her
    rigid, indrawn by a private gravity—
    her convex surface
    offers no toe-hold for analysis.
But perhaps the perfect smile—
    the self-assured sheen—
    her insularity's bright
    white carapace that shuns another's touch
    ask of you:
Is it her coolness or her cowardice
    (or are they one) that closes in-
    ward on itself
    denying entrance?
The probes of God's sharp grace
    his bruising mouth (and yours)
    threaten to broach her brittleness.
    And heaven's breath, hot,
    see how she shrinks from it
    on her ice palace
    as from all passion that seeks
    center
    in her hidden hollowness.

Not knowing she's destined for shell
    shock
    vainly she shields her vulnerable vacuum—
    postpones the breaking and entering—
    love's emptying of
    her chilly emptiness.

Shine in the dark I

From a dark dust of stars
kindled one, a prick of light.
Burn! small candle star,
burn in the black night.

In the still hushed heart
(dark as a black night)
shine! Savior newly born,
shine till the heart's light!

Shine in the dark II

Into blackness breached with white
the star shivers like a bell.
God of birth and brightness
bless the cool carillon
singing into sight!
Plot its poised pointing flight!

Dark has its victories
tonight, in David's town.
But the star bell's tongue
trembles silver still
in your felicity.

Shine in the dark III

The stars look out on
roofs of snow.
They see the night,
a velvet glow
with amber lanterns
shining so.

God searches through
the sweep of night.
Is there a heart burns
warm and bright
to warm God's own heart
at the sight?

to the municipal incinerator

among the perishables, go the
things of value, the shining cans, the plastic
forks, the occasional
alarm clock, assorted galvanized nails,
doll carriages, and dolls with most of their hair
left, machine parts and of course
odd shoes, applecores with sweet flesh on them,
frilled escarole, bones,
lobster shells, cartons, ashes, peelings, the decay
trapping the unspoiled parts, the untouched,
unused garbage of our lives, committing all
the lovely leftovers of affluence
to the sanitary engineers—
strong string, umbrellas of nine good spokes,
spools (naked but solid, clean, functional)
socks with only one hole, magazines
four weeks old and full as ever of wisdom and fact
and startling color,
cologne bottles of perfumed air, clear
as ice and less disposable,
and, in early January, Christmas trees
bared of everything but themselves,
and crumpled golden gift wrap—a bright heat
lying in wait for kindling

how many poets, soul
singers,
how many souls, how many brothers, how
many glistening minds, how many bodies,
how many eyeballs, hands, arms, quick black
feet, potent loins, fertile wombs, voices,
sinews, agile tongues, smouldering hopes,
hearts, proliferating brains
rot in the city?—refuse shovelled into
the disposal system, bound for some hot fire out of
sight out of mind—
the refused—I have refused you.
I have habitually ground
the dirty orange peel of your indignity under
my heel, and cursed you for littering
my mind's landscape

words were always my undoing
and now I have committed allegory:
looking for beauty in my own trash can
my God, I found truth

The Flounder

The flounder, (destined by birth to live and lie
miming the murky bottom of the sea
unlike the weathered fisherman, and me,
who much prefer the bottom of the sky)
jerked, raised resisting from its ocean bed
dark slabbed, a wet convulsion in the sun,
gills gaping, new existence but begun
will lie soon, on the gold beach, slimy dead.

And would another angler contemplate
hooking and drawing some defiant soul
up to eternity's unfiltered glare
swiftly, in that rare air, to suffocate,
blinded and gasping, helpless on heaven's shoal,
smeared with the scum of alien atmosphere?

Royalty

He was a plain man
and learned no latin

Having left all gold behind
he dealt out peace
to all us wild men
and the weather

He ate fish, bread,
country wine and God's will

Dust sandalled his feet

He wore purple only once
and that was an irony

Bloodcount

I

In summer the grey and amber
plasma of flying insects
sprays our windshields.
Milky blood of flowers drips
wet from their cut stalks. Maples
are cupped each spring for their sweetness.
Cactuses may be bled, too: a green gore,
a drink in the desert.
Not yet content, we tap our underground,
pick at dry veins in the dark, loosen
the black and silver clots,
pockmark the wilderness with wells

and unstop gushers to relieve
the hypertension of a continent.

And watch today's ghettos!
Look at all the gutters and gibbets of
revolutions. See the startling
color of death
at abbatoirs and all the battlefields!

The medieval medics did it often,
wiping away, maybe, as they sponged
the leechwounds
the thought of a bloodletting once done
in slow stages:
lash and thorn and nail and spear.

Look back further. Smell
the holiness of ancient altars, basalt piled
and varnished with sacrifice, drops
dried to a precious enamel over gold,
flecking even the feathered cherubim
while slaking
the thirst of justice between them.
Notice the smeared levitical hands,
the thumbs and the great toes of Aaron.

Think of the blood of the dead boys of Egypt.
Think of the dead men of Egypt: their blood
bottled within them, cool under water.

Now search
old doorposts and lintels
delicately patterned with hyssop
a sprinkling that signalled not revenge
but grace, printed in
indelible lambs' ink.

The evidence spoke once for Abel.
We listen to it
still.

II

How well chosen wine was
to stain our souls with remembrance!
He knew
how it burst, vivid,
from the flushed skins of grapes
grown for this sacramental crushing:
a shocking red, unforgettable as blood
a rich brew in the cup, a bitter
burning in the throat,
a warmth within
chosen well to etch on our lintels
the paradoxes of
a high priest bound to his own altar,
death as a tool of love,
and blood as a bleach.

Blindfold

When someone
pulls down a blind
shuts out seas
sky shore
other ships
shape
of the sun (though
warm still soaks down
blanket filtered)
floats a milky cataract
over every eye:
invisibles thrive and
foghorns celebrate.

In fact, unblunted
the overlapped
bass warnings
shaking the drenched air
above soft
incessant water-lap
sound doubly close
advertising their
unseen omnipresence
as though a new trans-
parency has settled
with fog
into all our ears.

new birth: heart spring

often after easter
last summer's deep
seeds rebel
at their long frozen sleep
split, swell
in the dark under
ground, twist, dance
to a new beat
push through a lace of old
pale roots

invited by an unseen heat
they spearhead up, almost
as though, suddenly,
their tender shoots
find the loam light
as air
not dense, not sodden cold

I saw a crocus once
in first flight
stretching so fast
from a late snow
(a boundary just passed
a singular horizon close below)
the white cap melt-
ing on its purple head

such swift greening of leaf wings
and stalk was clear celebration
of all sweet springs
combined
of sungold
smell of freshness, wind
first-time felt
light lifting, all new things
all things
good and right and all the old
left behind

Chance

Did God take his chances
on a son sent to fill flesh?
Was metamorphosis
a divine risk?

Once embodied
might he not find
earth's poignancies too sharp,
sweet flesh too sweet
to soon discard?
Might not man's joys
    (the growing
      of body mind and will,
      knowing
      companionship,
      the taste of shared bread,
      the smell of olives
      new-carved wood, and wine,
      morning's chill
      on a bare head,
      rough warm wool,
      a near, dust-blue Judean hill,
      evening's shine
      of oil lamps through an
      open door,
      day's work, tired muscles,
      a bed on the floor)
make up for his limitations?
Might he not even
wish for a peaceful death
from old age?

Ah, Father, but you knew
the incarnation was no gamble!
We are the risk you run.
Our destiny is not so clearly defined.
It's either/or for us.

And when I say you took no chance
on him,
he being our one chance of heaven,
I mean rather
once chosen, he's no chance
but certainty.

No backtrack, old Hansel

Age is a wilderness where your skills
   and your dry wit seem not enough
to find a path on pathless hills.
   Behind, you leave such fragile stuff—
such a sparse trail of shining stones
   shown by time's black birds to be bread
for scavengers. And no blank bones
   mark where your unfleshed dreams lie dead.
Nothingness is the harsh rebuff
   and age the wilderness where your will
and withered wit seem not enough
   to find paths on this pathless hill.

sonic boom

after this I'll be more careful
about stone-throwing in ponds—
specifically a small purple
one where even drowning gnats
make circles on the silver,
shaking its shallowness,
reaching its rim, swaying
the water weeds
who-knows-how-many
microscopic moulds
spread in the sun, on stumps, submerge?
how many algae, shredded, sink
to green slime?
what trauma follows
for a water flea,
one pebble-flung catastrophe?

27

Sweet light, sweet love, sweet life

Oh the sweet daytime shine on the earth!
Shadows only rub at its bloom.
    H'm. Yes, they agree
cocking upward pedagog's eyes, blinking
after the inside darkness.
    Yes, the sun is our
    source of energy.
    Light waves of regular
    length and intensity, diffused to
    some extent by atmosphere, are re-
    flected or absorbed by earth's irregular
    surfaces
    to produce a visual image and
    trigger chemical reaction. Light,
they continue, warming to the subject,
    may be refracted into the colors of
    the spectrum, red
    orange, yellow . . .
Stretching lazily, I murmur:
    Sunlight brightens the green of grass
    and makes water gold.
    I see it red, now, through closed lids.
    It warms my skin.

They see our hands together, the
electric touch of
skin to skin.
They know so much. They nod:
    A predictable human response;
    pure physical
    attraction;
    hormones at work!
    polarity;
    a biological urge.
Together we laugh, not
looking at them:
    It's spring,
    we're in love . . .

Conscious of case-histories, dryly
they abstract this
new birth: Perhaps
   a form of wish-fulfillment;
   insecurity's need to be
   dominated: a sublimation; in
   any case, gross intellectual
   dishonesty; the easy way out. Some
categorize it
theologically thus: regeneration, sal-
   vation, conversion—add one more to the
   total of the day's decisions.
My tears are telling it for me:
   I am happy.
   Peace fills me.
   I am touching God.

too much to ask

it seemed too much to ask
of one small virgin
that she should stake shame
against the will of God.
all she had to hold to
were those soft, inward
flutterings
and the remembered sting
of a brief junction—spirit
with flesh.
who would think it
more than a dream wish?
an implausible, laughable
defence.

and it seems much
too much to ask me
to be part of the
different thing—

God's shocking, unorthodox,
unheard of Thing
to further heaven's hopes
and summon God's glory.

night through a frosty window

galaxies glisten
across glass

the constellations
crowd between
clustered frost beads
tangle in their
ice-bright fringes

inches from my face
sealed-in stars
play with the planets

two kinds of tingling light
touch fingers
kiss in my eye

focusing
near to far
to near
tells me
they are worlds apart

but
melted by a breath
see
again
now they all swim together
on the dark pane

Parabola

Yes, I am comfortable
here in the dimness
almost as quiet as a
quiet nursery.
This softened oblong's
white-satin-quilted
safe as a bassinet.
Hopefully you
have swaddled me here
against time and the chill,
cradled my old age
here in the hush of
the organ lullaby.
Are you afraid that
I'll waken and cry?
Like seventy years back
(when I was new
and you celebrated
my coming. Now
my going's the theme
for your congregation).

Once more the heads
come over me, bending,
bunched and curious,
your comments echoes—
"He looks so peaceful."
"—so like his father."
Do you think in this sleep
I'll waken? Listen—
I can't cry an answer
or cry to be lifted
or cry for feeding.
Listen—my stillness
says clearly enough that
my soaring's over
my weightless flight
in the hot white air
is done. My bird bones
will splinter, will split
in the hard earth after
such a bold arc.
You though I was going
up forever?
But gravity claims us
each, today.
My moving parts are
all stopped cold.
I am almost fetal
ready at last
for final gestation.
A dark maternity
will hold me, treasured,
in this new womb.
Kiss me. My face
is still intact. Lock
my watertight lid
against your feelings,
against your flight wounds—
your own re-entry.

light my candle

though
I am but dull wax
and a
dead wick
Lord, thou
wilt light my candle

seventh day

Come Adam, son, mirror of myself,
    walk with me, talk, tell me
        do you see over there (your heart stirring)
    the grey dawn-dappled foals, ungainly,
        galloping down the brow of the world
    (fresh cooled with milky light, and
        frosted with sharp first foliage below)?
How startled the bird is
    at their hoofs' unheard-of thunder!
She springs unthinking
        into her first fine tentative lonely flight
    splitting the unwinged space
        beyond this perfect hill.

And Eve, as the clean mist unveils
        the unscarred grassy slope,
        distills, drips fragrant from the twigs
    to water the primeval greenery,
        do you smell now, on the warm-breathing breeze
    the fertile flavors of my undepleted earth?
        damp subtle essences of unploughed plains?

Listen, you two, gathering bunches from my heavy vines
    (purple and green and swung from tender stems
    with fragile bloom unrubbed)
        do you hear ground-hogs rooting happily
        in the rich undergrowth?

Below you, down a dustless avenue of oaks
    greenwashed as this first spring
        cool runs the river. Does it delight you both
    poured from my palm into my finger's furrow?
Up through the water shines the unmined gold
        and the thin silver slivers of the fish.

But here and now on your mid-morning hilltop,
    innocents, touch
        each other's hands, hold, yield yourselves together
    and fulfill
    the ardent rhythm of the sun.
Bathe in the blue aisles of light over you
        and in them feel the farthest reaches of my love
    and urgent joy, in you.
Laugh with me! Join in my delight!

Now rest
        under my hand, which also rests today.
    For your strong answering pleasure in my toil, my
    touch, is my contentedness.

The celebration

We might well
feel sorry for the
elder brother.

All he gets for his pains is
promises—promises,
a firm reproach, a truthful telling
that virtue brings
its own reward
while in the ballroom
across the hall
the black sheep and all his
loud friends
think it a fine Homecoming,
dance, laugh, live it up.

The firstborn's lack is
he's only a brother.

He hasn't tasted
parenthood, hasn't learned
the hard way
that love, longing,
endurance, disappointment,
bitter concern
often flower in stronger love
and later,
a more merry heart.

We would hate
to wish it on him, but
he can understand
only if, someday, *he* has
a prodigal son.

Under the snowing

Under the snowing
the leaves lie still.
Brown animals sleep
through the storm, unknowing,
behind the bank and the frozen hill.
And just as deep
in the coated stream
the slow fish grope
through their own dark, stagnant dream.
Who on earth would hope
for a new beginning
when the crusted snow
and the ice start thinning?
Who would ever know
that the night could stir
with warmth and wakening
coming, creeping,
for sodden root and fin and fur
and other things lonely and
cold and sleeping?

on eating a cake all by yourself

as soon as she said
". . . so lonely. . . ."
I talked warmly
as fast as I could
about gardening and church
fellowship
and convenient shopping centers
and Red Cross volunteer work
and good TV programs and
the Friend Closer Than a Brother
and others more needy
than she.

then, depositing the flowered
cake tin
on the kitchen counter
(neat as the numeral "1") I
left

common ground

new dug, rail braced, young ash blond
fence posts span the frozen slope
wedlocked in pairs repeating down
the road and out of sight
but there's an older couple
sharing the upper view across the river
(he's beech, she's thorny
bramble) whose tops feather today's
frost fog, whose ranging roots
lodge interlaced in the lean soil
that also anchors milkweed ragweed
thistle sorrel dock

time tangled the two (branch
and toe touched, leg locked)
season shift and shadow color them
alike, green gold or grey
rain rinses them
westerlies bare their brows
snows sift over their stiffness
and a bleached spring sun
speeds their slow sucking
from a common spring

Perfect love banishes fear
I John 4:18 (NEB)

The risk of love
is that of being unreturned.

For if I love too deep,
too hard, too long
and you love little
or you love
me not at all
then is my treasure given,
gone,
flown away lonely.

But if you give me back
passion for passion,
return my burning,
add your own
dark fire to flame my heart
then is love perfect
hot, round, augmented,
whole, endless, infinite,
and it is fear
that flies.

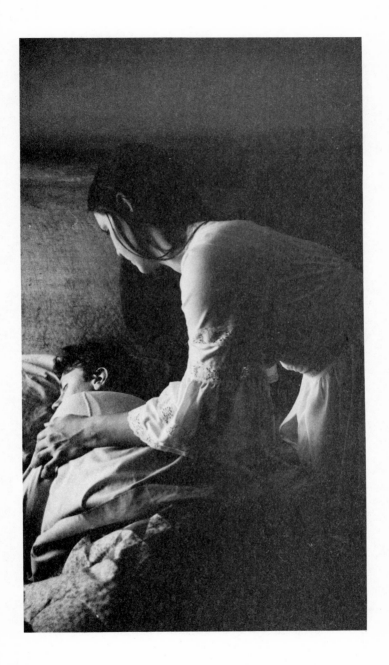

Small song

God of the sky,
God of the sea,
God of the rock
and bird and tree,
you are also
the God of me.

The pebble fell.
The water stirred
and stilled again.
The hidden bird
made song for you.
His praise you heard.

You heard him sing
from in the tree.
And searching still
I know you'll see
the love that wings
to you from me.

Steadfast taper
Job 28:3

His candle shines upon my head.
He trims the wick and guards the flame
and though the darkness creeps in close
the steadfast taper shines the same.

The flower of flame sways in the air.
Wind fingers snatch and try to snuff
the stalk his careful hands protect.
The light shines through. It is enough.

His candle shines on me in love,
(protective circle in the gloom)

and through the dreadful night I know
that he is with me in the room.

Throughout the weary waiting-time
the liquid flame shines thin and pure.
When tiredness dims my faith, I look
and see his light, and I am sure.

Maple leaf — Lisle Arboretum — Oct. 8

in the dry grey town we wanted
    woods to walk in

a bright random day
            giving us no reason but itself
followed us to the fringes
    (the sharp elbowed forest edges
        summerworn, windwarped, stooped
                to brown ground
    with defensive russet fingers)
pushed us through
    inside where
        even in a golden privacy of silence
    no long limbs bow

marvellous!
chance's afternoon must mark
    an exact midpoint for
            blonded maples
half of the brave yellow
        flags up there are
            loyally undetached—
        colorchanged but
            still brandishing
                ardent destines
half
livid underfoot

glowering up from infinite
overlappings:
          though sun sifts
                              slow
     and no wind breathes
     now
the air stir-fills with whispering
          tongues in a fire fall, a
          steady surrender
          flaming down through amber air
     under the thinning gilt of
               not-yet-falling stars

listen
is it better to burn breath-long
     high on a stalk
 or grounded
          smouldering
               a mulch of embers
     bedding fungus
                    moss
               leaf-mould
     maggots
          deadfalls
                    maple seeds?

we salvaged one
     bleached luminous, to warm
     winter in our town

Of consolation

It is down
makes
up seem
taller
black
sharpens white
flight
firms earth
underfoot
labor
blesses birth
with
later sleep

After silence
each sound
sings
dull clay
shines the
bright coin
in the pot
lemon
honeys its
sweet sequel
and my dark
distress
shows comfort
to be doubly
heaven-sent

Moses reclothed

Bare-soled he waits,
bowed bare-headed, stripped to the heart,
eyes narrowing, hands to his face
against the heat,
watching

Hissing, the dust-dry leaves
and cobwebs shrivel
baring the thin curved thorns
woven with gold
and the black-elbowed branches
wrapped in a web of flame
(An incandescence brighter
than the burnished mountain
under the burnished sky)

Wondering he waits
in the hot shadow of the smoking voice—
observes no quivering flake of ash
blow down-draft from the holy blaze
none glowing on the ground—
Shrinking, himself, before the scorching blast,
he sees the unshrinking thorny stems alive
seared but still strong, uncharred
piercing the fire

Enveloped now in burning ardent speech
he feels the hot sparks touching his
tinder soul
to turn him into flame

A song for simplicity

There are some things that should be as they are:
plain, unadorned, common and all-complete;
things not in a clutter, not in a clump,
unmuddled and unmeddled with;
the straight, the smooth, the salt, the sour, the sweet.
For all that's timeless, untutored, untailored and untooled;
for innocence unschooled;
for unploughed prairies, primal snow and sod,
water unmuddied, wind unruled,
for these, thank God.

Singly and strongly, from each separate star
a brightness pricks the retina from far
to near. And for clear eyes to see
deep space and dark infinity
with an untroubled gaze,
give praise.

With both hands unjewelled and with unbound hair
beauty herself stands unselfconscious where
she is enough to have, and worth the always holding.
The mind perceiving her, the heart enfolding
echoes the unchanged pattern from above
that praises God for loveliness, and love.

Glory again to God for word and phrase
whose magic, matching the mind's computed leap,
lands on the lip of truth,
(plain as a stone well's mouth, and as deep.)
and for the drum, the bell, the flute, the harp, the bird,
for music, Praise! that speaks without a word.

As for the rightness to be found

in the unembellished square and the plain round,
in geometric statement of a curve
respond! without reserve
but with astonishment that there's for every man
one point of time, one plainly drafted plan,
and in your unique place
give glory for God's grace.

All this from him whose three-in-one
so simply brought to birth
from the red earth
a son.
All our complexity, diversity, decor
facet the gem, encrust the clarity.
So pierce you now the opalescent glaze
till all your praise
rises to him in whom you find no flaw.

Of elms and God

A glib wind sings.
Wide blowing branches
are gravid with damp buds
dropping thin
brown hulls like insect wings
into the choked gutters
and warm airs and showers
are smudging winter's hard-
etched edges
fuzzing the dark wood skin
with pale and pendant flowers
until the twigs are diluted
to the color of fog.
And now, all my green
thoughts about elms in spring—
a tender catalog—
are drawn together, seen

in this one tall and lovely thing
rooted in my door-yard sod.

Yes, it is easy enough
to talk about an elm, but how
do I find words for God?
Spirit is not so readily trapped
in parts of speech
and to evaporate him to an abstract
is too simple, and not safe.
My verbal reach-
ings for him, like worn and
cast-off clothes, fit
him badly. He escapes them
undefined. They are not filled.
He is not found.
But if God sent to me
one signal from
himself—
if he distilled
his deity—
I would be bound
to take his Word for it.

New view

window-
framed, this new day—
full of light, leaves,
surprises, silver roofs—
is presented in
living color
by a new sponsor;
living sound, too,
if we believe
the loud birds.

Exit

When you go will you
go with a sizzle—
a spiteful spitting on a
hot plate,
a jig of steam?
with a crystal sigh on a beach
to leave a bubble?
or will your trickle
run, thinsilver,
to the open ocean?

When you leave will you
leave with a bang—
exploding like a
far star,
kicking your
hot cinders in God's eye?
or quietly, clinging
to your black match-stick corpus
a slow blue shrinking
in the dark?
or will your bud of burning
lift, bloom bright,
to a wider light?

Moses:
Psalm XC

Remember
the slave shack?
the rush bed
on the river?
the pagan palace
which was your
splendid prison?
the dust
of Midian's deserts?
the skin tents?
the wanderings in
a wilderness
walled in with thirst
and unthankfulness—
pot-holed
with graves?

Remember? How
could I forget, Lord?
yet always You
have been
my dwelling place.

"... for who can endure the day of his coming?"
Malachi 3:2

when an angel
    snapped the old thin threads of speech
            with an untimely birth
    announcement, slit
    the seemly cloth of an even
            more blessed event with
  shears of miracle,
    invaded the privacy of a dream,
multiplied
    to ravage the dark silk of the sky, the
            innocent ears
      with swords of sound:
news in a new dimension demanded
    qualification.
The righteous were as vulnerable as others.
    They trembled for those strong
    antecedent *fear nots,* whether goat-
        herds, virgins, workers in wood or
            holy barren priests.

in our nights our
    complicated modern dreams rarely
        flower into visions. No
        contemporary Gabriel
        dumbfounds our worship, or burning,
    visits our bedrooms. No
  sign-post satellite hauls us, earth-bound but
  star-struck, half
      around the world with hope.
Are our sensibilities
    too blunt to be assaulted
        with spatial power-plays and far-out
    proclamations of peace? Sterile,
  skeptics, yet we may be broken
        to his slow silent birth

          (new-torn, new-
             born ourselves at his
                beginning new in us).
His bigness may still burst
       our self-containment
    to tell us—without angels' mouths—
fear not.

God knows we need to hear it, now
        when he may shatter
        with his most shocking coming
    this proud cracked place
and more if, for longer waiting,
           he does not.

Explorer

You think you know my map.
You've pioneered my wild
prairies, charted all my rivers
and other
bodies of water,
travelled my highways and
hidden paths.
Yet now, when I decide
to dam an old creek or
cultivate an acre or
grow a small forest
do you feel, maybe,
lost a little?

Two answers to poverty

Along strict curbs and
over the cautious grass,
generously
the layered leaves are flinging down
a thousand polished keys
to their silvery city.
Choose one. (Each holds
the shining secret of maple trees.)
Turn it in its dark lock
for future fortune. Now
it glows in one bright thought
but, come autumn, its opulence
will ransom some of us.

The grass is captive.
How can it fill a city
with sun's splendor?
And dandelions (spring's
most useless bounty, but
lovely for glancing)
gave away all their coins and got
toothless old age for it.
Pick one. In the grey beard
is gold. Mind blows it away
but next year
the yellow millions
will glitter for you too!

Dial-a-prayer

On and off all day I've tried.
I can't get any answer.

Was I calling
a wrong number?
Is he out?
I'll try once more—
check in the big book—
dial, carefully.
A busy signal! Could
God have left his receiver
off the hook?
(Someone's at the door.
They'll have to wait.)
Dial "O".
"Operator—is this number
still in service? Yes?"
Spin it again. And still
no answer. I'm
positive my line's not
out of order. (Will
that knocking never stop?)

His phone rings on.
Easy for him to say "Need help?
Call on me any time!"
What if I can't get through?
What if he's gone?

or could that knocking be
him
calling on
me?

Open
John 20:19, 26

Doubt padlocked one door and
Memory put her back to the other.
Still the damp draught seeped in, though
Fear chinked all the cracks and
Blindness boarded up the window.
In the darkness that was left
Defeat crouched in his cold corner.

Then Jesus came
(all the doors being shut)
and stood among them.

Seed

God dug his seed
into dry dark earth.
after a pushing up
in hopeful birth
and healing bloom
and garland grace
he buried it again
in a darker place

Twice rudely-planted seed,
root, rise in me
and grow your green again,
your fruited tree

Arrested
"All crossroads have given way to cloverleafs. . . ."
—Thomas Howard

In this chase
only he
knows all
the ins and outs.

I am so used to
crossroads—I
who always like straight-
forwardness, accepted
confrontation
and other absolutes,
trusted all traffic lights
submitted to speed limits
responded
to the red octagonal STOP
and stopping
believed the old road markers
pointing, plainly,
both ways.

I who never minded on-coming
cars, I who lowered my
headlights dutifully,
find no felicity
in these new
concrete convolutions.
Risk is behind their
black banked pavement.
The subtleties
of multi-level loops
and one-way curves
go to my head in a blaze
of slick, a foliated
whirl of orange vertigo.

Fore and aft are irrationally
punctuated
with directional signals and
quick implacable squares
that shout NO STOPPING
and other orders I am going
too fast to stop anyway
faster than decision
and on this cloverleaf
luck has left me
alone in a snake of flight
over and over this
complex, evading
the straightaway
until his flashing eye comes
at me, up a ramp, catches me
near the sign that says
to him NO ENTRANCE,
EXIT to me.

Lucifer now

Breasting the word wind
nocturnal, sleek skinned
under star shifting, light lifting
sky talking, sun walking
slyly he slips
and slant eyed surveys
my thought thrusting, brain bursting
paining and gaining
soul spinning
at an idea's beginning.

When the words at its heel
congeal
he cooly stares
　　"What's so special and fine—"
silver lips grin, thin, dawn dim
　　"—about poems and prayers?"
Sweating I shout at him
　　"Special? fine? why, mine
　　is just born
　　and an answer is mine!"

February 24 encounter

blind and in the dark
and even after
the lit candle
(fire jumped to the wick
walked on wax)
sightless still
and dark
and still just as sure of
the safe dark

but what if
the burning
blazes through a blunt touch
to signal
new versions of light:
the sting
the singe and shrivel
oh—the smell of skin
over a quick flame!

The revolutionary

Do you
wince when you hear his name
made vanity?

What if you were not so safe
sheltered, circled by love
and convention?
What if
the world shouted at you?
Could you take the string
of hoarse words—glutton,
wino, devil, crazy
man, agitator, bastard,
nigger-lover, rebel,
and hang the grimy ornament
around your neck
and answer
love?

See the sharp stones poised
against your head! even
your dear friend
couples your name with curses
("By God! I know not God!")
the obscene affirmation
of infidelity
echoes, insistent,
from a henhouse roof.

Then—Slap! Spit! the whip,
the thorn. The gravel
grinds your fallen knees
under a whole world's weight
until
the hammering home of all
your innocence
stakes you, stranded,
halfway between hilltop and heaven
(neither will have you).

And will you whisper
forgive?

Equation

Now that the air has cleared,
the horizontal fringe of a
line of far fence
delicately divides
my snowed field
from a sky full of snow

But the dead pine
(whose stark geometry
bisects that faint
boundary)
transfixes both sky drift and
frozen foreground—
links them again with one
dark stroke
adding up for me the seasonal sum:
white + white = winter

Mary's song

Blue homespun and the bend of my breast
keep warm this small hot naked star
fallen to my arms. (Rest . . .
you who have had so far
to come.) Now nearness satisfies
the body of God sweetly. Quiet he lies
whose vigor hurled
a universe. He sleeps
whose eyelids have not closed before.

His breath (so slight it seems
no breath at all) once ruffled the dark deeps
to sprout a world.
Charmed by dove's voices, the whisper of straw,
he dreams,
hearing no music from his other spheres.
Breath, mouth, ears, eyes
he is curtailed
who overflowed all skies,
all years.
Older than eternity, now he
is new. Now native to earth as I am, nailed
to my poor planet, caught that I might be free,
blind in my womb to know my darkness ended,
brought to this birth
for me to be new-born,
and for him to see me mended
I must see him torn.

To know him risen

Is it obliquely
    through time's telescope, thick-
    lensed with two thousand Easters?
Or to my ear in latin, three chanted
    'Kyries' triumphing over a purple chancel?
Or in a rectangular glance at sepia snapshots
    of Jerusalem's Historic Sites?
Can I touch him through the cliché crust
    of lilies, stained glass, sunrise services?
Is a symbol soluble?
Can I flush out my eyes and rinse away
    the scales?
Must I be there?
Must I feel his freshness
    at an interval of inches? and sense, in-
    credulous, the reassurance of warm breath?
    and hear again the grit of stone
    under his sandal sole?
    those familiar Judean vowels
    in the deep voicing of beatitude? recognize
    the straight stance, quick eye,
    strength, purpose, movement, clear command—
    all the swift three-day antonyms of death
    that spring up to dispel its sting,
    to contradict its loss?
Must I be Thomas—belligerent in doubt,
    hesitant, tentative, convinced, humbled, loved,
    and *there*?
Must sight sustain belief?
Or is a closer blessedness
    to know him risen—now
    in this moment's finger-thrust of faith—here
    as an inner eyelid lifts?

to a young suicide

you always walked the edges
of the world
like eggshells
afraid
of your own weight

you nibbled at life
wrote novels with no
endings, dropped courses
in mid term, wore smooth
your records' outer rims

only once you
took a bite of God—and spat him out
he was more than you could swallow
like a tough rind
like all your half eaten apples

letters you wrote were never sent
(I would have read them)
often your face was censored
your laughter flat
even your dreams were incomplete

today
at last
your silence became pure
your escape final, finished
full (you can't be half dead)

for you
death offered
no samples
only this huge and
bitter pill

Hundredfold

Yesterday
(after first frost, with maples
blazing beyond fringes of stubble hay)
my husband and my sons
pulled up dead summer's stalks of corn
laying them flat among the weeds
for ploughing in again when next spring's born

I'm glad I picked the green tomatoes
two nights ago
and spread them, newspapered
to ripen on the basement floor
good company for the corn relish, row
and golden row in jars behind the closet door

Yes, I'm very glad
something's left—something not dead
after.all the hilling and hoeing
seeding and sprouting, greening and growing—
after the blowing
tassels high as a woman's hands above her head
>   *Corn relish for Sunday dinner—grace*
>   *the days when outside snowings*
>   *whiten winter's face!*

Let me leave fruit
(but not in someone's basement)
when I grow browned
and old and pulled up by the root
and laid down flat
and ploughed into the ground

Absolute-ly

If roads went nowhere
and rain fell dry,
if birds crawled low
and worms flew high,
if faces were flat
and the midday sky
looked always dark
and the sun shone square,
if beauty were costly
and God unfair
if densest earth
were as thin as air,
if clocks went backwards
and grass grew blue
and lions were happiest
in the zoo
and five were the sum
of two and two
would you be me?
might I be you?

How would we *think*
if all sprouts grew down
and the sea churned pink
and the clouds turned brown
and God's face were fixed
in an awful frown?
I'm thankful, I'm thankful
(are you too?)
that grass is green
and sky is blue
and the sun is round
and fact is true
and we can count on
gravity,
and God is good
and beauty free

and, for the sake of
our sanity,
that you are you
and I am me.

The bright side

why is it
always such a surprise
when good erupts
from bad?
you should know—
trouble seduces sympathy
like when
you broke your leg
and boys
swarmed bee-like
with autographs
to sweeten a heroine's
plaster

next time
please *expect*
to charm stars
from snowstorms
butter from
sour milk and
daffodils
from mud

". . . for you are a mist"

James talked about transience.
Noticing
a spider's web under the olive trees
splendidly hung with early drops, already
vanishing up the vortex of the air
perhaps he saw there all his grandest schemes—
the purity of Israel's infant church
the apostolic councils
solemn conclaves
policy declarations and decrees—
a trivial display to heaven's wide arch
all to be sucked away
into one brilliant plan—not his.

As he saw the rain
stinging the earth into a fruitful green
then smoking, steaming up under the eastern sun
surging away in
farewell to the parching plain
he must have sensed his own stern, sturdy life
(condensed at birth under that human skin)
now gathered in him, waiting
the inevitable evaporation,
the final up-draft that would leave
his muscles dry, his strong bones prone
and his dark skull a shell.

It may have been a palestinian dew
(sparks among thirsty grasses)
showed him the simile,
or Jordan at dawn, a flowing amber
sending up a veil to blot the sun.
Did he ask himself—Christ's brother—
    What is my short span?
    a heaven-sent refreshment? or a curtain
    cutting out the light?

And I must ask it now
(small moisture that I am)
under the sun of God's great grace on me:
    Which am I—dew, or fog?

Graveyard

Hard stars of glass, mosaic on the rocks
dropped from jagged window frames, green-chipped,
reflect the cruel sparkle of the sun
into the darkened hollows. False shifting light
that witchlike, plays inside the battered roofs,
reveals a tatter of upholstery,
shifts with pale glee, transmuting to fools' gold
the tortured metal and the rotten rust.

Thin digits of yellow grass caress
a chalk blue fading chassis, tenderly.
(Deceptive tenderness! The slow blue burns.
The thin blades are the flames
from the hot breath of years.)

Sunday morning

Why does the doxology always
    have to be pitched so high?
    We pay the organist enough. He should
    know better. Why—
    there are the Winters'. They haven't
    been out in months. I'm amazed they'll
    show their faces, even now—
    the rumors I've heard!
Now a psalm is being read. It is a
    long psalm. David got
    rather emotional at times.
    Exaggerated, surely? No sense of perspective.
    No *restraint.*
    I see they've put in the stained glass at last.
    Very effective, that combination
    of rose and purple.
Ah, the pastoral prayer.
    We cross our knees the other way.
    Warm, isn't it?
Eyes earnestly closed now . . .
    Someone may notice our sincerity.
    All the other heads are nodding
    at the right angle.
    Hands piously postured. Amens
    intoned with just the right proportion
    of reverence and fervor.
The Offertory, and the clink of change. Don't
    tell me! I forgot my check!
And now the Sermon. *Sanctity*
    and Twentieth Century Society.
    Stimulating I hope. Sanctity is *so* necessary.
    I must talk to Pastor about this
    red plush. It's wearing thin.

At last—the Benediction.
    Well, he went overtime, as usual. My leg
    has gone to sleep.

Hat on straight? Friendly now—
"Oh, Mrs. Winters. Delightful to see you again!
The prayer and missionary meeting?
Yes, Tuesday. It *will* be a relief to get out-
side, won't it? So stuffy
in here.

First flurry

The white on the windshield
is, variously,
organdy-flocking; stars
stuck on a sky; (a cold cliché
but see, there they are,
poised and six-pointed,
plain as night!)
asterisks, footnoting
with soft insistence
the sweeping syntax of
new wiper blades;
blotting paper soaking up
stop light signatures
marked on melting streets.
Of course
all I'm seeing is
November's first flurry.
I'll feel differently
about falling snow
next March.

Tithes
Matthew 23:23

All in bunches the furred leaves
are hung—narrow and stiff and
greyer than they grew
under the wall—
starred with a few
dry seeds. I've crushed and weighed
a small part of them into God's pot,
spikes, stalks and all.
The sun drained all the green
they'd got.
All they can give now is a tithe of death,
a thin spice in the air. But has God seen?
Has he the nose to savor
the last fine fragrance of their breath?
Will caraway mask my justice—
make it seem fair? Can mint
sweeten a meager mercy, or a hint
of dill improve the flavor
of my faith? Why ask? It's his affair—
and his prerogative to bless or not to bless.
The love he wants is too wide for my inches;
his righteousness
too heavy. And like the sun, not just a tenth
but "all", he says. "With all your heart",
and that's nine-tenths too much!
(Such burdens and my good intention fails.)
I'll stick to weighing herbs on garden scales,
and my white-painted wall is thick enough
I think, to keep out conscience, questions,
critics, seekers, friends, rough
beggars and itinerant carpenters,
though I suppose
God could leap it if I asked him to
or if he chose.

Made flesh

              After
the bright beam of hot annunciation
fused heaven with dark earth
his searing sharply-focused light
went out for a while
eclipsed in amniotic gloom:
his cool immensity of splendor
his universal grace
small-folded in a warm dim
female space—
the Word stern-sentenced
to be nine months dumb—
infinity walled in a womb
until the next enormity—
the Mighty, after submission
to a woman's pains
helpless on a barn-bare floor
first-tasting bitter earth.

              Now
I in him surrender
to the crush and cry of birth.
Because eternity
was closeted in time
he is my open door
to forever.
From his imprisonment my freedoms grow,
find wings.
Part of his body, I transcend this flesh.
From his sweet silence my mouth sings.
Out of his dark I glow.
My life, as his,
slips through death's mesh,
time's bars,
joins hands with heaven,
speaks with stars.

Step on it

All these broken bridges—
we have always tried to build them
to each other and
to heaven.
Why is it such a
sad surprise
when last year's iron-strong
out-thrust organization, this month's
shining project, today's
far-flung silver network of good
resolutions
all answer the future's questions with
rust
and the sharp, ugly jutting
of the unfinished?
We have miscalculated every time.
Our blueprints are smudged.
We never order enough steel.
Our foundations are shallow as mud.
Our cables fray.
Our superstructure is stuck together
clumsily
with rivets of the wrong size.

We are our own botched bridges.
We were schooled in Babel
and our ambitious soaring
sinks in the sea.
How could we hope to carry your heavy glory?
We cannot even bear the weight
of our own failure.

But you did the unthinkable.
You built
one Bridge to us
solid enough, long
enough, strong enough
to stand all tides for all time,
linking
the unlinkable.

Night's lodging

Across the purple-patterned snow
laced with light of lantern-glow,
dappled with dark,
comes Christ, the Child born from the skies.
Those are stars that are his eyes.
His baby face is wise
seen by my candle spark.
But is he cold from the wind's cold blow?
Where will he go?

I'll wrap him warm with love,
well as I'm able,
in my heart stable!

forecast

planting
seeds
inevitably
changes my
feelings
about
rain

air craft

wind is your
flight pattern

you have wings that work
and a real beak and
no wheels

you are not made of
rivets and sheet
metal: shafts of air
backbone your light
lapped vanes

floating: your straight stems
lie flat against your fan
and when you stand stiff
on sand and salt frost
they are bare
ends of the wires that
firm your flesh

you are
soft as sky and stern
as sea

your markings are
international: grey
and white for the
world's clouds and black-
tipped dark
as all stormy water

laced with lightning
you are bow and arrow both
shooting yourself
up at infinity

but your aim fails:
falling your path drops
and folds clean as a wave
I love you

the sun shines through
your edges: you have eyes
for windows and you light
lightly on this pier and
look at me
as if God made you

Coins

Straitened for centuries between his banks,
ironed smooth by the blue weights of air,
yesterday's shining river
broke again into a thousand wrinkles.
Not age, nor strain but
summer's reckless breathing
captured the careless gold
and spread it prodigally edge to edge
stolen, new-minted
from the sun, to my delight,
by rebel water, spendthrift wind.

Stiff breathless oaks
guard the flat face of channeled grey
glass, misted, docile again, blindfold
under this next morning's
stifled sky. And I'm no Midas.
All the gold is gone.
(But for a few pennies' worth of
shine I've hoarded—locked away
from the sun's claim.)

Freeway

The split sky should have been
    sign enough. Clean and unclouded, gold
    filled the east and warmed my face.
    Arching above, the slate sharp-
    fronted shadow outpaced mine, the heavy speed of snow
    only a sullen threat until
    first flecks, erratic, isolate,
    fling down a hissing challenge on the glass,
    flake faster, a bright diffusion blunting
    the asphalt edges, bleaching away
    all burning blues, muffling
    the brass coin still
    indistinctly glinting in its pouch of sky,
    thick flocking the curved crystal,
    a wall of falling stars, a flying
    fog of white and thicker white
    and white thin as a thread
    and then the grace of a grey
    shape standing, single-footed, in a deepening drift,
    brow brushed with white, as snow blind as myself,
    dumb but definitive—"MAXIMUM SPEED 65".
It might as well say 90 (or 20)
    now that there's no bite
    through to the black bone of the road,
    no boundaries, nothing but one
    half-smothered sign to show
    the shoulder-frontiers of this space
    (a valley filling up
    with furious purity,
    a splash of whitewash for the world,
    clean covers endlessly unfolding
    for my chrysalis.)
Snow blanket? stopping here to wait
    I may as well pretend I'm warm.

Ever green

topped
with an earth-bound angel
burdened
with man-made stars
tinsel bound
but touched with
no true gold
cropped
girdled with electricity
why be
a temporary tree
glass-fruited
dry
de-rooted?

when you may be
planted with purpose
in a flowered field
and where
living in clean light
strong air
crowned with the repeated gold
of every evening,
every night
real stars may nest
in your elbow
rest
be found in your shade
healing
in your perennial green
and from deep springs your roots
may suck enough to swell
your nine sweet fruits

Lord, come and see

Their crying primes the human wells in him.
(A baffled grief, of women just like those
who, after the days of triumph song
and savagery,
will wait, frustrated, at another tomb,
hands full, hearts empty as the hole
bared by the heaven-hefted stone.)
This bursting in him—this is how they'll feel
after the common fate—be born to die—
has smeared him too, like Lazarus here.
He knows they think
he'll be the grand exception to the rule.
But burial gauze, tenderly layered,
bulky with herbs,
must bind his own man's flesh awhile
where all men darkly go.

He too must dare decay,
shut in to the ministrations of worms.

Damp, new-dug hollowness from Joseph's cave
(a private echo back from time-to-be)
shivers the core in him
and loving Lazarus, who must die twice,
he weeps.

Stronghold

This shell clasps my core so strongly.
Fortress or trap?
Whichever, it's well built
corporeal, functional, tough,
and all its gaps
are either

essential holes (to keep,
hopefully,
the prisoner alive and tantalized
via lungs, eardrums, eyeballs
by the out-of-reach)
or slits in the stone that
forestall my
lover's embraces.

Bird in gin or buttressed maiden—
how should I view myself?
A gloating "Aha, you can't escape!" or
a crenelated, moated, armored rebuff
from behind a raised drawbridge?
And outside—huntsman or suppliant?

But perhaps it's nothing so medieval.
Perhaps it's just a soft pink
brickwall, round, high enough,
without handholds,
so that the universe straight up
is ceiling for my heart, frosted over
with stars and suns and falcon's
feathers.
(Beam, flicker, pierce. I find I'm not
invulnerable to thoughts. Such shafts
come closer than the impatient one
inches away on the outside.)

What's needed, of course, either way,
is a breach in the wall,
a crack, so that mortar falls in clots
and naked clay splits
under his plundering
which also springs the trap.

Miracle

A muddy corm
(encouraged by
a south wall and a warm
wet silver shower)
will glow
topaz, in a crocus flower.

Let April show
more wonder—
out of those soft, dull clouds
lightning spears thunder,
living storm
dissolves grey shrouds
of snow,
brown blankets of shaggy sod
turn emerald.

        Why doubt?
The sullen reprobate,
the sodden clod,
the heart of hate,
the darkened face,
the old,
watered and warmed by grace
may sprout
and grow up green and gold
for God!

Tryptich

The sun shines through you
splashing your primary
color hot all over
the altar and the pews
stamping the prim, primitive
shadows of your Passion
on the bare wood

Christ—you
and your Apostles
are up there so stiff
paralyzed in the
gothic frame
their tears futile, frozen
gems in black settings—you
a captive of glass
caught by the nails and the thin lead

you who have surveyed
our centuries
with translucent benediction—
you who have been held

high and almighty
in a web of metal
your angular atonement
colorfully captured for worship
outlined for adoration—
you whose crystal halo holds no
light of its own behind the thorns—
break your two-dimensioned bars
come down to
where we are
kneeling, drenched in your artificial red

come to us out of your
high stained window
not your shadow, not your bright symbols
but yourself—
if you be Christ
come down

Out of the woods

Through the woods he found a way
bordered with bogs, rocks, reptiles,
thorned and fruitless boughs
Dark knowledge (he being all alone
his God face wet with man sweat)
dripped with the heavy fog
from the forsaken sky to shaken earth, and
into his constant heart;
a two-armed trunk, cross-branched,
the landmark of his mind
as through the olive trees he found a way.

I tread a track too. But in my dense woods
valerian and vagabond vines
leaf over hidden pricks.
Odors of pine, bird songs, enchant the sense.
Comfort of cushion moss, dim shimmering
shade for sleep, or velvet ways wind
invitation down the rich ravines
into deep groves for love
among the tender leaves.
Till, cruciform, new shadows touch my feet
as brightness beckons through the trees
falls in gold arrows on the forest floor
to point escape from the collective charm
the shameless sorcery
of these too lovely woods.

Reluctant prophet

Both were dwellers
in deep places (one
in the dark bowels
of ships and great fish
and wounded pride.
The other
in the silvery belly
of the seas.) Both
heard God saying
"Go!"
but the whale
did as he was told.

The partaking
John 6:53-56

Bread of the Presence
was
in Moses' day
served on engraved gold plates
to you and your select few.
And in exclusive glory
one alone and lonely man
sprinkled, with fear,
the ceremonial drops that pleaded
failure for another year
to you, known then
as only high and holy—
heavens apart
from common men.

Often we taste the
granular body of wheat
(Think of the Grain that died!)
and swallow together
the grape's warm bitter blood
(Remember First Fruit!)
knowing ourselves a part of you
as you took part
of us, flowed
in our kind of veins
quickened cells like ours
into a human subdividing.
Now you are multiplied—
we are your fingers and your feet,
your tender heart—
we are your broken side.

Take now and crumble small and
cast us
on the world's waters—
your contemporary shewbread.
Feed us
to more than five thousand men
and in our dark daily flood of living
pour yourself out again!

other books in the **Wheaton Literary Series:**

The Achievement of C. S. Lewis, by Thomas Howard. "Written with Lewis's own passionate power with words." —*Peter Kreeft*. Paper, 196 pages

Adam, by David Bolt. An imaginative retelling of the Genesis 1-3 narrative. "I think it splendid." —*C. S. Lewis*. Cloth, 143 pages

And It Was Good: Reflections on Beginnings, by Madeleine L'Engle. Personal reflections on the first part of Genesis sharing L'Engle's insights on the character of the Creator and the quality of his creation. Cloth, 213 pages

Creation in Christ: Unspoken Sermons, by George MacDonald, edited by Rolland Hein. Devotional essays revealing a deeply moving understanding of holiness and man's relationship to God. Paper, 342 pages

Geometries of Light, poems by Eugene Warren. "He shows how abundantly love has poured Itself into our 'seed-filled light' and 'night-locked flesh.' " —*Robert Siegel*. Paper, 108 pages

A Guide Through Narnia, by Martha C. Sammons. A detailed study of Lewis and his Chronicles of Narnia, with map, chronology and index of names and places. Paper, 165 pages

Images of Salvation in the Fiction of C. S. Lewis, by Clyde S. Kilby. Explores the Christian meaning in Lewis's juvenile and adult fiction. Cloth, 140 pages

Life Essential: The Hope of the Gospel, by George MacDonald, edited by Rolland Hein. "A book for those who hunger after righteousness." —*Corbin S. Carnell*. Paper, 102 pages

The Miracles of Our Lord, by George MacDonald, edited by Rolland Hein. "A better set of meditations on the miracles of Christ would be hard to find." —*Walter Elwell*. Paper, 170 pages

The Psalm of Christ: Forty Poems on the Twenty-second Psalm, by Chad Walsh. "I am absolutely delighted to discover this fusion of deeply held faith and the free working of a true poet's sensitivity." —*J. B. Phillips*. Paper, 80 pages

The Secret Trees, poems by Luci Shaw. "These are the real thing, true poems . . . they work by magic." —*Calvin Linton*. Cloth, illustrated with photographs, 79 pages

The Sighting, poems by Luci Shaw. "Few poets in our day can speak of incarnational reality with the eloquence of Luci Shaw." —*Harold Fickett*. Paper, illustrated with photographs, 96 pages

Tolkien and The Silmarillion, by Clyde S. Kilby. A fascinating view of Tolkien as a scholar, writer, creator and Christian, based on Kilby's close association during the collation of *The Silmarillion*. Cloth, 89 pages

Walking on Water: Reflections on Faith & Art, by Madeleine L'Engle. Shows us the impact of the Word on words and ourselves as co-creators with God. Cloth, 198 pages

The Weather of the Heart, poems by Madeleine L'Engle. "Read her poetry and be chastened and filled with joy." —*Thomas Howard*. Cloth, 96 pages

The World of George MacDonald: Selections from His Works of Fiction, edited by Rolland Hein. "A treasure of a book—one to be read and reread." —*Frank E. Gaebelein*. Paper, 199 pages

Available from your local bookstore, or from
HAROLD SHAW PUBLISHERS
Box 567, Wheaton, IL 60189